All The Best Things
Come In Threes
Personal Accounts of Hurt and Nonsense

To my parents.

I will love you forever.

CONTENTS

TRILOGIES

ACKNOWLEDGMENTS

Thank you to Liz and Heather, Dom, Eliot and Nic for proofreading this book and helping me to make it the best it could be.

Thank you to the incredible Honey Southworth (@honeylella) for capturing the essence of the book in the front cover.

Part 1
Thesis

Fatal Flaws

Thirst

Push
And push again
For you are thirsty

Though pure of heart
You move too fast
Push too far

Progress can push you off a cliff
Broken chains could release a monster
Some things should not be known

But you don't care
For you are thirsty
So you keep pushing

Fragile and Dangerous

Glass Machine Gun

I am dangerous
I am fragile
My bullets hit
My temper agile

Throwing stones
From a glass house
The impending fire
You'll have to douse

The bullets fly
And you get hurt
I do too
Which is absurd

But a glass machine gun
Is just that
The shattered glass
You can't take back

Monochrome

Darkness

The darkness overwhelms
Spreading from the inside out
A wave of unrelenting black
That from my heart and mouth will spout

I'm covered from head to toe
The darkness quickly thickening
I am my own worst nightmare
The void, to others, sickening

All who I touch are consumed
Their lives torn up by the awful dark
What's needed is an opposite
To change me with their light so stark

Healing

Shattered

Your beauty, your love
Weaponised
You strike me, I shatter
Atomised

You were a bat, a sword, a gun
And I was just glass
Shattered

In pieces, my worst fears
Realised
I loathe you, I hate you
Demonised

I felt safe in your hands
But I was porcelain thrown to the floor
Shattered

All my feelings
Minimised
Damage done
Optimised

Then you left me
A broken mess
Shattered

Forever and Always

Shattered

Freedom

The Cage

I wake up to the cold steel bars of a cage
This cage
My cage

I stare out at the dark grey walls
I listen to the rushing water
I taste the metallic clang in the air
This cage
My cage

Years sat in silence
Cross legged
Unable to move or live
This cage
My cage

I scream at the top of my lungs
How long have I been here?
Why was I put here?
Who am I?
Without this cage
My cage

The bars begin to melt away
Just like time itself
And suddenly there is nothing but me
No cage
My cage

Plant Life

A Lover's Torture

He loves me
He loves me not
She says as she hurts me

She loves me
She loves me not
He says, pulling me apart

They love me
They love me not
Their indecision kills me

For I love them all
But I'm stuck in their grasp
My petals plucked
They're breaking my heart

An Ode to Broken Friendships

Tendril

I reach out
For love
For support
For friendship
Only to be batted away

I retreat
Agitated
Hurt
Resentful
And I stay there for a while

Time passes
Lonely
Peaceful
Independent
For me to reach out again

I reach out
For love
For support
For friendship
And I find gold

I am a state

Liquid

When I relax
And I unwind
A liquid state
Enters my mind

No longer uptight
My thoughts flow
If I was not water
No one would know

I am water
Refreshing and smooth
My soul floats
Nothing more to soothe

Mind City

Garden

My personality is a garden
I water it everyday
It is constantly changing
And full of colour

My mind is a garden
Full of organisms competing for resources
Full of life
Delicate

My soul is a garden
Wild and green
Old and earthy
Striving for growth

Need Space

Comet

Beauty and ice
Shooting past
The brighter they shine
The shorter they last

Something to admire
But never to touch
He doesn't come close
Not that it matters that much

For we are to pass
Like ships in the night
You get away
Being Earthbound is my plight

Battery

Wind Up

I'm very easy to wind up
A perfect little toy
You grab the winder and twist
Something I cannot avoid

I'm starting to feel very tense
I think that this is you
The shame is you don't know my limits
Soon I'll be on the move

You have pushed and pulled and twisted
Didn't think that I would break
As I get ready to explode
You will realise your mistake

Society Sucks

Possessioned

You wake up in the middle of the night
Your possessions have possessed you
You're cut and bound by clothes and objects
What they want you have no clue

Finally the slave becomes the master
The clothes wear you that you once wore
Your fridge keeps coming in to stare at you
And then leaving, saying nothing more

Your various cables pounce like cobras
Wrapping you tightly in their grasp
You sink to the floor, overcome
You used them all, but now the time is theirs to laugh

Designated

Designated Driver

I'm in the driver's seat
And everything's fine
I'm where you've placed
But I can't drive

I do must best
I shift the gears
I hear a crunch
It hurts my ears

We're losing speed
And getting behind
I keep my eyes on the road
But I am blind

You shout from the passenger seat
And berate me for my driving
But I didn't want this
I'm barely surviving

No Homo

Close Your Eyes

Close your eyes dear
It will all be fine
I am the spider and you are the fly

Close your eyes dear
Just relax
Feel your body get stuck in wax

Close your eyes dear
Let us in
Fit into this box so we can win

Open your eyes dear
You'll see what's in store
The rug is not under your feet any more

Mood

We Stan a Queen

On a throne
In a crown
That is where you'll find me
I wasn't born royal
I didn't have it thrust upon me
I achieved it

Who doesn't stan a Queen?

Femininity
Is not a weakness
In any and all
It is a strength
To have the ability
To grow past pain

Who couldn't stan a Queen?

We stand together
Or not at all
We climb our mountains
That were never molehills
This is what royalty looks like
Don't look away

We stan a Queen

Part 2
Antithesis

Fatal Flaws

You can do it

You can do it
But I cannot
As you can run
Where I just stop

The skills that you
Always possessed
Surpass me
Even at my best

Your own self-doubt
You did not plant
As you can do it
But I just can't

Fragile and Dangerous

Imploding Bomb

I've pushed myself too far
I'm over the cliff
Watch out below

Time ticks as I fall
The penny drops
I'm terrified

When I go I'm taking you with me
When it happens
And I implode

I'll draw you in
Close to me
And crush you

Monochrome

Light

The order of the light
Their role is to ignite
The fire within us all
To stop the darkness looming tall

That does not mean, though
That we are all as white as snow
As in some the darkness does persist
So we must fight when it insists

The world will all be light again
One day the bad will end and then
There will be no need to attack
But for now we must keep the darkness back

Healing

Melted

As the light of day breaks I begin to melt
Like a candle under heat

My body drips and drips and drips
A puddle; sticky, bittersweet

I say goodbye to my resolve
Floating slowly on the wind

Breaking down was not my goal
But this way, my worries I rescind

I breathe a deep sigh of relief
And at once I feel my body slide

Closer and closer to the ground
My pieces I no longer need to hide

Only look and never touch
As if you do you're sure to stick

To the puddle on the floor
Who melted down so sadly quick

Freedom

Free

At any moment
You can look around
And suddenly
You'll be free

I crawl along the pavement
Such a shame my legs have atrophied

I breathe in the fresh air
But my lungs do nothing now for me

I would take in the lovely scene
But in the dark my sight did flee

All I can think of my newfound freedom
Is what a total travesty

The scars destroy my living
This suffering my destiny

But worse still than the physical
The mental scars that folks can't see

All now that I can stand to think
Is that I miss my cage, my protection, my security

Plant Life

Necessitree

With the weight of the world bearing down on me
Oh how much easier
To be a tree

Just like a nymph in ancient times
Real and permanent
With others intertwined

So here I stand with arms outstretched
Will branches come?
Will I find my best?

Trees breathe and exist in peace
They make the world better
So humans won't cease

My time has come to leave the pain
Become a tree
Go home again

Leaves start to sprout out of my head
My fingers elongating
My roots start to spread

So here I stand and mark the day
Of a tree
Whose worries have all gone away

An Ode to Broken Friendships

Parasite

We are equals
Acting as one
Two lion cubs
Fighting against the parasite

I turn my back
And look away
It seems we have won
Goodbye the parasite

A short-lived victory
As you have vanished
I look on my back and see you
The parasite

I bite and I tear
To get free
From my bitter enemy
The parasite

Bloody and wounded
I scratch you and hurt myself
Because it's me
The parasite

I am a state

Solid

I try to be a solid friend
From the beginning
Until the end

I always try to do my best
Standing up
To support and protest

We have to all build up our souls
As you can't pick at something
With no holes

Mind City

Graveyard

My mind
Is where ideas go to die
A mass grave of unidentified projects
Killed by fear of failure

The gravestones are large and looming
Their shadows all encompassing
Many things have been lost there
Buried to avoid the light of day

This graveyard is scary and peaceful
For what is buried here has come to rest
It is not a busy place
You will not be disturbed here

Need Space

Collision

When we collided
My heart stopped
My lungs collapsed
A porcelain doll
Crushed by a brick

Every action has its equal opposite
But we were not equal
I was weak
So when we collided
The full force was mine to bear

As when a comet hits a planet
One is destroyed
The other barren
I do not know who is worse off
Or further still, who the comet was

Battery

Sunlight

I like to sit in the light and stay
Watching all of my thoughts drift away
A moment I can take to breathe
No need to move, my heart's at ease

I feel the grass and see the sky
And in its beauty I wonder why
I ended up being angry at all
My stress and chains all loosen and fall

I am a cat, absorbing the rays
If only I could do this every day
But the world insists on progress
So for now I'll just soak up and de-stress

Society Sucks

Social Construct

'Fit into this box,' she said
But he did not like the box
It was not comfortable
So he built himself a new one
One with space to stand and stretch
One where he was not crushed by expectation

'Blue is for boys and pink is for girls,' he said
But they did not understand this
Because they were something altogether different
So they built a house
And painted it green and purple and brown
An expression all of their own

'You can't do that,' they said
But she felt she could
And that she should be able to try
So she built a crutch, some stairs and a ramp
And she climbed them
Because she felt she could

Designated

Designated Healer

My team needs me
I am the healer
I do not have much power, or toughness, or strength
But when someone needs me
You know I will go to any length

I'm not a fighter
So if you don't need a doormat
I'm not your guy
But I'll be there to pick up the pieces
And lift you up so that you can fly

But this can create problems
Everyone leans on you
And sometimes they don't see
That if I get wounded
Who is going to heal me?

No Homo

Indignant

The colour on my nails is offensive
Apparently

They tell me I'm going to hell
I tell them I'll see them there

I pray to God and follow his word
Heavenly fire has not rained down on me yet

If I am an anomaly
They are boring

If I am a logistical issue
Then they need better problem-solvers

I'm just here to love freely
Until I can I will remain indignant

Mood

Dancing in a Burning House

The fire rises
Consuming all
Everything is wrong
It's everyone's fault

The plates are broken
Eyes teary
My heart is weary
But my skin is oaken

As things are all falling apart
I can't help but smile
I will celebrate
That I am still alive

So I will dance in a burning house
Until the roof comes down
When the walls crumble
And we can't dance anymore

Part 3
Synthesis

Fatal Flaws

Not Your Owner

If someone hurts you
You do not have to do what they say
They are not your owner

If you are thrown out in the cold
You do not need to stay
They are not your owner

You owe them nothing
You are not useless
Cut the cord
They are not your owner

Fragile and Dangerous

Blunt Dagger

A blunt dagger can be useful
Despite its perceived flaws
It could be ceremonial, sentimental
Or just help you with the chores

A dagger that is blunt
Does not mean terrible
It could be a letter opener
Or perhaps be very wearable

Without its primary cause
It does not cease to be
It holds the value
Of whatever you see

It holds many a purpose
Once left unfulfilled
By a perfect dagger
Used only to kill

Monochrome

Greyscale

The darkness and light are colliding
All I see is grey
Everything is good and bad
That's how it should stay

It's there to differentiate
Between the highs and lows
A blurry moral middle ground
Without which nothing could be known

Here we all live in the grey
That is where the world resides
Light and dark together
Working to improve our lives

Healing

Repaired

There I was
Broken
Shattered and melted

Utterly spent
Lethargic
Wilted

But over time
The puddle
Hardened

My shattered heart
My feelings
Pardoned

A seamstress
Sowing me
Back together

As being broken
Is not
Forever

So here I am
Soggy and
Cracked

But better that
Than
Too broken to act

Freedom

Ball and Chain

It has been a long while
Since I escaped my cage

Freedom is a funny thing
At least time now passes with my age

My scars have begun to settle
And with every step I have improved

Stockholm Syndrome holding on
I try my hardest to remove

Every step I took was so much lighter
I felt that I was moving on

But freedom is never an easy process
And this a light did shine upon

So every now and again
When you see me walking free

You might still hear a jangle
Or a dragging of steel right behind me

For though I am much freer now
I drag a ball and chain through every age

But when all is said and done
It's much less restrictive than the cage

Plant Life

Venus' Trap

I have felt great pain
So pain I shall cause
Because I am a trap
So I take no pause
In taking captives
Maybe one or two
They cannot escape
What can they do?
So I keep them
My only friends
As I am a plant
I can't make amends
My body a fortress
With people inside
No one will find them
The best place to hide
But something strange
Is occurring

I'm getting hot
The tides are turning
The last man I trapped
He had a knife
Too late I realise
He fights for his life
I am cut open
Two people hop out
I am defeated after
After a successful bout
So I lay there
Sad and bleeding
I should've been better
Instead of deceiving
So a good resolution
For a plant that is dying
I'll be better next time
No killing or lying

An Ode to Broken Friendships

Out of Sight

If a tree falls in the forest
And no one hears it
Where does it go?

When you turn off a light
And leave a room
Does the furniture disappear or stay?

If out of sight
Is out of mind
What does that make me?

If we played hide and seek
And you closed your eyes
Would I vanish?
A figment of your imagination
A fleeting puff of smoke

You keep your eyes closed to spite me
I do not exist
Is this what it has come to?

I am a state

Gas

Free as a bird
Riding the wind
Light as a gas

A free spirit
Unconstrained
Living the life

I go higher
Through the clouds
Unstoppable

I don't have wings
The sun could melt
I am air

Mind City

Home

When you are weary
You can always come home
For even when you are not here
You are held in my heart

I am comfortable here
In my own mind
After years
I am at home

My arms are open wide for you
You're always in my mind
For what is mine is also yours
This was always your home

Need Space

Dust

The dust will settle eventually
What rises must fall
So what is unsettled
Will settle again

My feathers are ruffled
My hackles raised
They will be for a while
Or longer

Comfort is the goal
You do not make me feel comfortable
But the dust will settle

As it happened before
So it will happen again

Battery

Drain

I'm not feeling low today
Just tired
And that's okay

I had fun, my mind is spent
It's time to rest
Restore the dent

Doing things is a trade
You spend your energy
And wait for it to be repaid

I live my life like a fiesta
So now it's time
For my daily siesta

Society Sucks

Inside/Outside

The inner circle is full of users
Draining people
Cheats and abusers

One wrong step and you are out
Dignity removed
You've lost your clout

Being locked out can be confusing
But soon you'll find
That it's amusing

Although the outside is a foreign world
Freedom there
Is grown and learned

People on the outside rarely return
To the inner circle
Once self-worth has been earned

You were once on the inside
But now you are not
It's much more rewarding to build your own slot

Designated

Designated Scapegoat

It is my fault
I take the blame
I've lost your trust
It'll never be the same

It is not my fault
But that does not matter
I will fall on my sword
Just to make this all better

It is your fault
But I don't mind
You've done this for me
You've been divine

So it is my fault
And that is okay
We'll get through it
To fight another day

No Homo

Fabulous

Started from the bottom now I'm queer
Void of any kind of fear

I know parts of what I'm meant to do
God has perfect plans for me and you

For out of bruises comes redemption
An amazing feeling, not our invention

For you could be me and I could be them
But we would do badly and problems would stem

So I celebrate all of God's creation
No mistakes, just different stations

So we stand and live tumultuous
Here we come; the queer and the fabulous

Mood

Sobbing Into My Coffee

Some days it is all too much
So I go and get a coffee
Or a mocha
And I sob
I listen to sad music
To spice it up
To push the tears out
I tell myself
That it's good for my skin
But really
It's good for my soul

Printed in Great Britain
by Amazon

58394304R00037